BODY OF WORK

BODY OF WORK

TINA CANE

VELIZ
BOOKS

velizbooks.com

Handwritten inscription:

18 June 2019

for Lain,

So wonderful to
meet you
in Soho.

Thank you
for coming.

Tina

Veliz Books' titles are available to the trade through our website and our primary distributor, Small Press Distribution
(800) 869.7553. For personal orders, catalogs, or other information, write to info@velizbooks.com

For further information write Veliz Books:
P.O. Box 920243, El Paso, TX 79902
velizbooks.com

ISBN: 9781949776027

Cover art Alberto Giacometti "Tête de Cheval," 1951
© Alberto Giacometti Estate/VAGA at ARS, NY
All rights reserved

Cover design by Silvana Ayala

TABLE OF CONTENTS

REALITY SERIES

Reality Series 11
Luck 22
Life Hacks 23
Post-Its 25
Greenwood Cemetery 26

(MY) AMERICAN JOURNAL

(My) American Journal 31

(Y)OUR AMERICAN HOUSE

(Y)our American House 73

WORK

Some Kinds of Fire 83
Beauty Mark 84
Work 86
Systems 87
Handwork 88
Ballad 90

Flowers   95
Symbols   96
Mother   97
Marriage: A City   98
House and Home   99
Youngest Son   100
Daily Beast   101
What He Said From His Hospital Bed   102
Hack   103
Jamming   105
Body of Water   106
Conflation   107

NOTES   109
ACKNOWLEDGEMENTS   112
THANKS   113

REALITY SERIES

You can close your eyes to reality but not to memories.

—Stanislaw Jerzy Lec

REALITY SERIES

I

today
on Sixth Avenue

sports coat-
junkie-man

on the same oldschool
skateboard as ever   ragged

wheels but a beautiful
deck   wood smooth

as if the plank had been
tumbled in the sea

his right leg
a manic pendulum

skinny-looking
but strong

under thin
jeans   hard to believe

he's still
around

after all
these years

II

nine days
into thirty

and already
a gray hair

that won't sit down
that springs up

from under
my palm

in the morning
in the mirror

a kind
of private joke

time marching on

III

once my bedroom
caught fire

in summer
orange flames

floated up
like feathers

exotic hypnotic
messages

I stood staring
several seconds

when the lights
went out I found

the dog but the cat
would not come

from behind
the mantle mirror

fragile as china   she
knew she wouldn't

make it   in the flashing
darkness I saw

my smoky
silhouette

backing
out of the room

IV

in the bathroom
on Tenth Avenue   pink tile

and a view of Hell's Kitchen
my mother pierced

my ears with a needle
and thread   I cried

in rage but later
admired the loose red

loops when each
wound had healed

and was studded
with a dot of gold

V

my mother's mother told
me not to wash my hair

on those days
on those days

she said shaking
her head   the natural

balance of oils
in the scalp

is disturbed by water
its atomic opposite

that pale lather
strips and the sweet

masking scent of *Breck*
can throw the body off

throw the body off
she said *don't*

throw your body
like that

VI

106 men
in a village

were taken
to a barn

and shot
last month

an old man
in a wool cap

told
the story

to the news
putting

each man's
photograph

on the grass
for the camera

he said the names
of the men

not stopping
even as

the lens
moved away

VII

a friend once
booked a red-eye

first-class
from Helsinki

in the middle
of the night   leaving

her sleeping husband
unaware   sardonic

as ever
as they lifted

her to the stretcher
so she wouldn't miss

the plane   seat on the aisle
meal intact

cut tumbler
of ice glinting

bright next to the mini
cutlery on the plastic tray

frantic the whole way
making calls to old friends

from 30,000 feet
she tried to trip the Queen

of Sweden on her way
to the bathroom

time froze
as she watched

the Queen fumble
for her crown   failing

to fall down or find
humor she vanished

through a folding door
marked vacant

At Long Last, a New Sun
With a Family of Planets

~*The New York Times*, April 16, 1999

LUCK

There was a time   when I'd say things like   *That shit broke*

about a toaster I had   or something in a story I had read   and the boy I'd be with

would laugh and shake his head   like he couldn't believe his luck   or some such

feeling I still can't name   but which broke me a little all the same   the way we do

at different times   when we are young   or not so young   how we cleave

ourselves open to see inside   to find some luck in the story   to believe it

LIFE HACKS

Take a picture of business cards   people hand you   in case you lose it

Before you throw a *post-it* away   run it in between the keys on your keyboard   to collect crumbs and fluff

Use a coozie to cover your stick   on hot days

When taking a picture   squint your eyes   to make your smile look more genuine

Put pancake mix in a ketchup bottle   for a no-mess experience

Doritos are great for kindling   if you can't find any

Wrinkly shirt?   Throw it in the dryer with a few ice cubes   wrinkles gone!

Freeze grapes to chill wine   without watering it down

Put a wooden spoon across a boiling pot   to keep it from boiling over

Rub a walnut on damaged wooden furniture   to cover up dings

When you want to cross words out   that you don't want to be legible   write random words over the original

Put a blue ink cartridge in a red pen   because no one steals a red pen

Turn on your seat warmer   to keep pizza warm while driving home

Use a clothes pin   to hold a nail   whilst hammering

Do something unusual when locking the door   before a long trip   to remember that you've definitely done it

Almost finished your jar of *Nutella?*   end it with ice cream

POST-ITS

: fill pink eye prescription   : eat prawns in red sauce à la Tilda Swinton   : savor the subtle resistance of a thing

perfectly prepared   : pick up dry cleaning   : tumble in a dream of adulterous Milanese gentry   : eat fried chicken

that is not sad   : keep grease in a coffee can   : call Mrs. Thacker   : quell panic attack sparked by *Bananas Foster*

Yankee Candle conversation   :write some checks   : flip three shifts of chocolate chip pancakes by 7:26 a.m.

: labor over love of a thing that does not love you back   : love it all the same   : write a poem   : right a wrong

: loathe the sound of your own voice   : loathe your mother's voice within your voice   : loathe it in the car

: refuse to get a dog   : loathe it in the kitchen   : make tea   : make nice   : make the bed   : make a dental appoinment

: take out the recycling   : recycle old rumors into a new narrative   : scrap that   : make supper from scraps

: call it "breakfast dinner"   : eat toast hunched over the sink   : think a complete thought in a dream of resistance

: refuse the right to recycle adultery   : refuse sad love scraps   : labor over chocolate chips   : love the right dog

: spark a new narrative   : tumble with Tilda Swinton   : love the wrong poem for the right of your voice

: savor the emotion in toast   : toast a sound perfectly prepared   : love the Yankees   : love the Milanese   : love it all

GREENWOOD CEMETERY

Brooklyn, New York

I had to use the map   and proximity of lanes named for flowers   *Magnolia   Lily   Marigold*

to guide me to his spot   the lots were poorly marked   and the markers didn't correspond

        anxious at times under a strong noon sun   I stumbled in divets of turned earth

stopping to observe   the apparatus of straps and plywood boards lying in wait   to lower another coffin to its grave

alone amid acres   of grass and granite markers   none of them his   I heard my father

urging me   as I grew thirsty and damp with sweat   to just leave

and head for Chinatown

        It's enough that you were here   he said

but how could that be   and how could his name

have been so faintly engraved   without my seeing until now

running my fingers over the stones of his neighbors   *Hernández   Ricci   Genovese*

I felt certain   they stood more ready to rise   in relief against the elements   to hold

the snow and water   in their depressions until spring

(MY) AMERICAN JOURNAL

HORSE

A day will come
when someone appears
grateful, saying
— Come in
and sit at our table.

— António Osório

(My) American journal   catalogue of grievances and valentines

condolence archive   store of sudden joy   my continuum

veritable as the journey my grandma made was long   a road whose song I know

almost nothing of   but that the chickens in the mountains   had their throats slit that the soldiers brandished   bodies on their swords   my mother told me that

the Japanese took everything they know from China   our food our silk our tongue each iota a stolen etymology   stuck in the throat of her history   as chains

a distant aunt swallowed to save from invaders   her entrails twisting

with mineral jade   as she died under a stand of white pine these are stories I was told to believe   to make (my) American journal complete   I hypothesize

that a British officer in Hong Kong   is the father of my mother's brother   how else to explain

the silence the strangeness and the shame   or requisite papers obtained   how endlessly these people evade   no tree to trace   no leaves to place   in rows along the sideboard

I grasp truth like I cup fog   whole zones dissipate   as soon as I show up

as if the continuous mysteries are me   not for the solving   but quintessential a cliffhanger   American as a reality show   I grow into myself   mixed product of multitudes

glorious bastardization   *for amber waves of grain*   and footprints on the moon

are particulars portrayed as proof   of a manifest dream which counts me among its *vigorous Americans*   everyone journeyed here to make it so   my grandfather

marching down Mott Street mid-winter   in a plain white tee   defied the cold

as he strode several paces ahead of the family   his lips blue   his jaw set tight as grit they kept a fresh television set unopened in its box   under the kitchen table   while the one we watched

displayed everything in green   needed pliers to have its channels changed   but it hadn't died so everything wrung within an inch of its life   is comfort of a certain kind   stoicism in a land of plenty

is one kind of shrine   without the candle and the donut on a plate   daily they made space for the dead crowding out other essentials while   protecting the wall by the stove with sheets of tin foil

to guard against oil from her spattering wok   my grandmother kept the enamel of her *White Rose* stove

unflecked as a temple floor   pulled racks from its oven without mitts   I used to wonder if she still had fingerprints shrine to my ignorance this journal of (my) American   for I *am* American   vigorous in manifestation

prone to hypothesis and imagination   terrible with maps I lack any sense of direction   often I think my car has been stolen when I step out of the post office into the sun   my eyes screw up in the brightness   only to spot my car down the block

where I left it   so many types of theft   I get why a woman would swallow a necklace   but not the television in the box waste is one thing want another   even as I stash half-price shampoo under my sink   always on the verge of running out

is a tendency I keep   so privately even my husband doesn't see   this vestige of poverty   were we ever that poor

wasn't there (almost) always enough   of what it means to be from here   the USA with its pyramids and three squares a day it's okay to dream a little dream   of shamans and technology   but the pragmatist in me shuns decadence

metabolizes pride like an outsider   sees hypocrisy in a miniskirt   but I'm alright with two sides

of a dime   (my) America (my) journal (my) thighs

my own mother was married in go-go boots and a veil   so many variables

the frightening energy of being alive   and all that immigrant striving   no time to stop until the galaxy shows up   when the lights go down at the Hayden Planetarium   I am eight

and unprepared for the vast celestial   possibilities of another realm   sacred as any home

I had known   inexplicable as any tenement or punk hotel of painters   my parents put us in no stranger to violence   the strange violence of children walking   with their hands on each other's shoulders

single file as they flee their schools   is still new to some Americans   but not to young Americans

We live just these twenty years and die for fifty more   performing the *extremely uphill* work that is talking

to ourselves as Americans   what justifies my hunger

for other ways of life   hasn't America been mostly good (enough) to me   like the '80s

like boyfriends like luck   why grandmother placed a fork and a *Coke* beside my rice bowl

why she praised my almond eyes   their hint of occidental   unfortunate passport but also worldly shape of disgrace   which she said men preferred   already implying a darkness   whereas

I had heard blondes   my fondness as a child for Marilyn   was a shrine to beauty and sadness

a photo of Monroe in glasses   reading by a window   taped to the wall above my bureau because she liked books like me   because neither of us spoke Chinese   because love

is a function of catch and release   as every family is a galaxy   and every galaxy is others (my) mother's love was deep   unsparing as cosmic law   noble and flawed

a supernova of dark matter   spinning light and heat   my whole life

I traipsed the *unloved streets* of New York   retracing the implosion   of our catch and release

to say there's nothing left in Chinatown for me   is to revisit its particulars   the heaps of trash on every corner   the rivers of fish blood running into its sewers   I once saw a couple of Napa cabbage

propped against a fire hydrant   like a pair of pale jade sentinels   but that package bound for California stuffed with silk and gold   appeared when I was ten years old   when my grandparents told me

that an uncle had had a baby boy   light began pouring from the open box   as if the power of the gift

of being male   was an astral happening   happening in a kitchen on Mott Street   I was dizzy from the dazzling rays   bouncing off the foil-covered walls   the blinding revelation that

my almond eyes were a prize   this boy would never need   that being born to a hippie mother from the Midwest

still bested being me   the daughter of a daughter and a *lofan*   my dad used to laugh at *paleface* and *white devil* whereas I wanted all the variables lined up   on my side of the ledger   never good at math

too often give me half and I am happy   a true American   here among the roses and the rot grows a plot that also raises me   a pen that writes before it dies   a machine-made candy

landscape with two thousand kinds of cereal   plus corn dust to scuff up   with the gun in my boot proof that I am American   is my callousness   I care but how much   do I spare anything

with which I am reluctant to part   possessions are one way to chart a life   among mine is a nativity scene

in which everyone is Chinese   I thought every country had its own Jesus until I was five   today I cherish time small god of possibilities   and poems that think   plus genre of allegiance to American things   like running

from the past   like cross-pollination and desegregation   so many bees so many boys   dying in the fields and streets so much beauty and goodwill squandered   as in the gesture of a single rose   botched valentine

who knows why so little goes as planned   why so little planning goes into anything   any more than I can inherit the Earth   can America be my father   like money banked beneath a mattress

I hoard memories   half the time they're not even mine   we are alike in this way   like the man

who lost his wife driving home from a party   when a horse crashed through their windshield   killed her dead and left him unharmed with his hat still on his head   that man was a father   your father and mine

and the woman your mother and your sister   do you get where I'm going with this   again with the deer and our collective memory of apples   a common dream of lightning   and the phantom family

I've lost   just as my husband's long ago hair catches air   when he rolls down the window

does my every move tingle   with activated absence   yes and the broken simile of it is (my) imagination   that will not put the horse back in its stable   or hair back on the head

that moves not to fix the clan   for there are answers   but not a lot of questions   any more than I am made of what I am afraid of   then you are too   so get this   the truth is of no consequence

to me   personal mythology   that most American language of anguish and anxiety   lacks privacy as lost an art   as fireflies in a mason jar   as lucidity itself

that we quit hoarding and collect ourselves   and find other kinds of conservation   disrupt

no language with pain   that we reclaim permission to dream a dream   dreamy and permissive as America enchanted as land revised over time   rooted in lack   like every aspiration   seeks power to pressure a form

how the storm left every twig   on every branch encased in a layer of ice   how nature entered my life snow melting in the Green Mountains   makes a rushing sound in spring   how my father recounted this same scene

standing on the corner of Church Street   I couldn't explain   that I wasn't ready for the snow

or for anything else   or how now I am   almost ready for everything

(Y)OUR AMERICAN HOUSE

(Y)our American house   is a monument to industry   a *tender age facility*

with a skeleton of wood   white house brown hands   any punk hotel

of painters my parents put us in   rent control is *in the way of my life* the way

Warhol temperament and strife   tenement rationalizations   and gentrified stabs at stabilization

can be a place to hang your hat

my bones are not happy today you say   the box of bones

in the basement are bird   I say the skull on the shelf   jaw of jackal   artifice and artifact national or otherwise   a house is not a *Walmart*   a box is not a shop   my babies want me home

geography is luck   or the story of a toaster   some shit you can't believe   how they used to give

toasters away for free   at the bank of all places   with checking *&* savings   but if you want free lunch you need a plan   to open up show up   you know what I mean   be vulnerable make nice(r)

if you want to build a home   you better believe   the boy you're with   will hold together not break   you into pieces like some   all strapping dumb luck rolled into one

nation under one roof of stars

a common constellation for all

WORK

Most of us have jobs that are too small for our spirits.

—Studs Terkel, *Working*

SOME KINDS OF FIRE

                    Anna Akhmatova burned

her poems and the light of Madrid was like water

at *La Latina* luncheonette I ate a cup of chocolate

and a motor oil *churro*

every day for a week

recovering

                          the cherry bomb alley that was our street

Hotel Chelsea ablaze from a rum-soaked pillow and a cigarette, 1977

iron balconies were dropping like lace

windows were popping like sobs

Can you describe this?   someone asked

Anna Akhmatova

as she stood in line   *Yes*

she said   *I can*

BEAUTY MARK

I am standing in a stance of memory

to recapture *Chapultepec Park*   kaleidoscope

of candies   carts of cut mangoes   a museum of gold

down in Oaxaca
                    girls circled the *zócalo*   arm in arm

wearing thick glossy braids   and dresses of pressed white cotton

how the heat brought out   lovers and elders and the beauty

mark beneath my right eye
                    which emerged like a sun print or a sign

point on a line leading nowhere   except where I was

which was Mexico   whose giant bugs scattered for cover

across the ceiling when I flipped on the light

just off the night bus   stumbling with fatigue   I had fever dreams

of hands moving over me as I slept   with the lamp on   my head under the sheets

I woke at sunrise covered in sweat   my own salt on my brow and lip   as if from hard work as when *two shores refuse to touch*   as when lapsed love is as much

diffidence as distance   or how the beauty of a place   exerts discreet pain

to make its mark indelible

WORK

I can't stop horses as much as you can't stop horses
"Other Horses," Michael Klein

What is work   but a horse is a beast   to be one with the broom   I bristle

toil tool and trade   work is a poem I made   is my children is family a broken

phrase difficult to say   with a mouth full of teeth   sore from grief is another

kind of work   or driving long hours through the night   only to start each day

in its middle   Spartan with a sparse meal to break the fast   a private kind

of penance one man makes   while another says   *We use water to start over*

how Baldwin used snow from the Alps   to write his way back to the Harlem

streets of his youth   whereas Debbie from Seekonk   says *I'm Switzerland here*

meaning you can tell me anything   and I almost do   keeping the most arduous

parts of the work   to myself *for* myself   sometimes comparing

my heart to a horse   sometimes *fast & beautiful*   often beastly

& burdensome   with my six shades of brown in each eye   I see work

in every corner of the earth   the way work always finds me where I stand

list in hand   a clover in my pocket

SYSTEMS

for Matthew Zapruder

What is work   but a system   a solar-powered family

or animal of poverty   whose hunger taste of metal

is a tendency to hoard

                handed down   natural as disaster

like work within trees   secret language   a system of roots

the oldest machine   of reciprocity and need

                    is my mind

the grid off which I live   that my mind might also be a tree

or a hummingbird   freed from its cage   my trill tinted

rose with nectar   aglow   amid the aura of Etruscan women

who thrill   at the songs I make   of their aches

and appetites   each refrain   a wheel within a wheel

a music of lineage   ancient as math bright as grass

HANDWORK

Lucid dreaming is not a job   but a steady occupation

I do not have a big dream   they are only little dreams   and right now I cannot think of one

My father read the paper   while my mother scrubbed the floor

I pay a woman $100 a week to help me keep my house clean

I forget to rinse the rice   because I am rushing

I wipe the counter   and wipe the counter again

My son makes a mountain of suds in his hair

I rinse behind his ears

Women balance large bundles of sticks on their heads

I forget to rinse the rice   because I am rushing

I wipe the counter   and wipe the counter again

For ten years I fed my children from my body

Kissed their fists to custom make them milk   to fight the germs

I did this without realizing   I did it all the same

I wipe the counter   and wipe the counter again

If I had to live under a bridge   my children would go with me

When my daughter asks me to brush her hair

I use fragrant oil   so that in a perfumed dream

she will remember me   with steady hands

hands that wipe the counter   that sometimes rinse the rice

BALLAD

Night of my mouth

dry with stardust

light of my children

breaking through

my own mother

kept me close

'til she did not

for every should

be crying thing

no one said a word

silence was an engine

greased with non-speech

until my body

like every woman's body

became a time machine of blood

or milk on which to grow

my children   each his own

separate flame

each a flicker

of stardust in my palm

forgiveness how they

crunched the gears of time

forgiveness how they

howled their passage

to meet me how

my body was made

to be a knife

their bodies

knife-like

clashing with me

in the darkness of me

until we broke

through the light

of our arrival

with fresh tenderness

for giving

how tender

for them I can be

that they find tenderness

in the world

outside of me I say

if Medea can be an actress

wearing *Pumas* in Brooklyn

I say I can

be a mother too

if that most modern

staging of this

most ancient rage

is nature my ferocity

it's no tragedy to me

that with equal parts

eternity I split

myself in three

pulling each body

through the dust

of star dust

in my throat

a reticence I mistook

for motherhood

as if motherhood

all silent shoulder

to the wheel

all mouth to breast

of milk is not also

a golden lasso

science cannot break

or replicate

for spangled ions

know every baby's

first song

is a ballad

with her mother

sung from the other side

FLOWERS

I swear by all flowers

that flowers are work

sometimes *fast & beautiful*

handwork   the rough heart

of a grassy-eyed rose

kindred spirit to the tree

SYMBOLS

Back when *egg creams* were still a thing   and loving trees was just not possible   I'd order a *lime ricky*

through the window at *Dave's Luncheonette*   still on the corner of Houston and Canal   back when Curtis Sliwa

still had a wife named Lisa   who wore her red beret on the subway   with lipstick and a Jujitsu pout

It was a time I dreamt I was a fire escape   that I escaped fires and I did   get on a plane to see a boy in Spain

eat falafel on a bench in the *Marais*   while reading the plaque on *Rue des Rosiers*   about Jewish children sent

to Buchenwald   I rushed from quai to quai at *Gare du Nord*   but never found what I was looking for

Back when smoking was still my thing   I smoked anything I could find   until Rothko filled me up

a blank pillow was almost enough   but even then television was a barrier   a useless *neutralizing ray*

that if you'd point it at things   still wouldn't make them go away

These days I keep a suitcase of letters I don't read   I drink wine in the evening   and watch my kids

chase rabbits in the hedge   I comb my children's hair with my fingers while they sleep   pressing each to grow

together strong and flexible   a stand of bamboo

MOTHER

Work is a mother

as I am a mother

the mother of her

leaving is me

art of losing

art of story

poem of mother

is mother of poem

is me

MARRIAGE: A CITY

Bike sharing in the big city is one expression of *elegant density*

or an *elaborate situation*   as one man once described a piece of music

and the woman's voice within it   it's been said *a woman needs a man*

like a fish needs a bicycle   a riff on man needing God   which he may

as a fish may need a bike   if she lives in the city   as a man may need a dog

careening down city streets   we pedal without helmets   unpracticed against traffic

on borrowed bikes   all *do as I say not as I do*   but I do   need a man need a bike

need to voice my *elegant density*   for the *elaborate situation* is me   a music of need

                                        as my city is need of a god

HOUSE AND HOME

I can't stop houses   as much as you can't stop houses

every home is a monument to industry   every house has a skeleton of wood

I clear our refuse from the landing   the cobwebs from the bones   write

the poem that lives in my head
                      just as the bed wants to be made the poem

just as the sheets need to be cleaned the poem   home of living desire

house of creatures who require   my touch the poem   just as daily love

aches to be sung by night the poem   all demand and appetite the poem

each day I trill industrious   a hummingbird poem of mothering   my nature

the poem insists upon my presence   exerts upon my children the poem

in my throat on waking   and at night   when I take to my bed the poem

in my head
            unstoppable house and home of poem

YOUNGEST SON

We used to laugh and say   he was *naked and flying around with the stars*

before he came down to be with us   these days he says   *When I was dead*

because *naked* means sexy   and he's not a baby   knows what sex is

would rather be dead   but I don't want the word dead around my kids

or around any mother's son   so I say *Honey, you were never dead*

and he says   *Then I fell like a raindrop*   *into your mouth* and I say *Yes*

how the other morning I said *Yes*   when he called fog   *a cloud on the ground*

how he was formed   is forming   from rain in my mouth   just as one day

I believe he will *go out for sweets*   *& come back*   just like that

for some boys like him   it may be that easy   to not be a cloud

called back to its rain place   for salt tears not   to fill the space

left in his wake

DAILY BEAST

I commit to reading accounts of the torture before the beheadings

as a form of emotional engagement with world turmoil   a juncture

at which to decide   which side of the dream I am on   one side being

to study the invention of women by men   by which I mean   to understand

women as men's vision of the female version of themselves
                                                        mistakenly

I typed *remale* just now   flickering on the screen   another side of the dream

to remake things   to put the head back on the body   to commit to reading

loving   accounting for
                    the body of each man as my own

WHAT HE SAID FROM HIS HOSPITAL BED

(what I heard)

You have to write

so your children know

who you are.

HACK

He left his hack license on the bed-stand   with the pocketknife

we gave him   reluctant to renew   in case he didn't make it back

there was a wall of books by his bed   stacks of articles he would have read

had he returned to spend the $65   on a photo of his eyes squinting

into the middle distance   of the gaunt days ahead

it's said   that every unworn shoe in a closet   represents a unit

of work   a mark of time wasted   or money earned   but however

you look   a shoe is a shoe is a shoe
                                        An embarrassment of riches

my dad always chimed   as he ripped open his gifts   at Christmastime

when he finally let go   they gave me his belongings   in a clear plastic bag

that read *Belongings*   I couldn't carry his clothes   while also carrying my baby

in my belly   down into the belly of the train   I took the buckle from his belt and put the bag in the trash   on the corner of *Lexington Avenue*

then caught the downtown express   empty-handed   brass in my pocket

unable to end   even this poem   the way I want it

JAMMING

I tried jamming the brand with my body   but my body wasn't enough   it took

my pre-existing family   the one living poem I've made   for me to be seen

through the lens of the men at the helm   and were it not for my family values

a collateral self   I keep safe in the cleavage   of my brain I would remain

invisible   just jamming to *Chic* in my kitchen   in a fanny pack and pregnant again

but don't judge
           the '80s were good to me

in their way   aside from trickle down and crack cocaine   it was a time

of total freedom   for which I keep reaching back   any dose of nostalgia

to defend against   this savage present day   vague ache of middle-age

which I hear is an illness   not an interlude   in the music of time

but my tune   has always been a hook   that *if you can't be free*   *be a mystery*

pre-existence means life   and brand loyalty is just proof   of a love of disco

BODY OF WATER

Swimming is   *sex and death and thinking*   and these things mean the world to me

so don't let my heart be brief   let me stick with this   how water with its perfect memory

holds my nostalgia without weight   lets souvenirs take shape   without resistance

composed as a buddha   if I'm lucky   enough I float like a strand of DNA   in a body of water

displacing that water   whose origin mythical as my love   of olive trees and baklava

is not ancestry   but an appetite traced to crescent pastries   from the Poseidon Bakery

back in Hell's Kitchen   and why not   speak   as a family which we did

of those cookies with a fondness   reserved for some relative   who had ground down the almonds

with her own bare hands   but there was no such relation   so let me stick with this   vision

in light of our difficult histories   like when Orlando said *Same Calvary*   we were talking politics

but I saw hooves   charging into a stream   they flooded my mind   the five men who jumped

his brother in Flagstaff   so they could smash his jaw with a brick   sex and death

and thinking   how a memory of near-drowning   tunes the body to tread

CONFLATION

What you give me   is vision and trees

everything happens to you   happens to me   one form for another

a wishbone on the windowsill   is the small stand of pines

through the window   is *Jenny's Woods*   childhood kingdom

of a girl and her brother   home of birds   home we built

how a man who dies of drink   is a man who dies of thirst

how if I am love   I am not   always the loving one

how if I stay   I am also   sometimes running away

                    same as you same as anyone

NOTES

p. 27: "(My) American Journal" owes a debt to the essay "Nothing Personal" by James Baldwin (Dell Books, 1964), which prompted me to write this poem and whose message has not let up.

p. 27: The title "(My) American Journal" alludes to the poem "[American Journal]" by Robert Hayden.

p. 29: "Horse" by António Osório, translated from the Portuguese by Patrício Ferrari in collaboration with Susan M. Brown, "Selected Poems," *The Broome Street Review*, August 2017.

p. 38: *vigorous Americans* comes from the poem "[American Journal]" by Robert Hayden, *Collected Poems of Robert Hayden*, Ed. Frederick Glaysher, Liveright Publishing.

p. 49: *We live just these twenty years and die for fifty more* is a line from "Heroes" by David Bowie.

p. 49: *extremely uphill* is how James Baldwin characterizes speaking to Americans in his essay "Nothing Personal," Dell Books, 1964.

p. 54: *unloved streets* is borrowed from the essay "Nothing Personal" by James Baldwin, Dell Books, 1964.

p. 71: The title of "(Y)our American House" makes reference to a remark by John Lewis during an interview on CNN during which he called America "our house."

p. 73: *in the way of my life* comes from "China Girl" by David Bowie.

p. 77: *should be crying thing* comes from "Epigraph," by Nikki Finney, used with permission by the author.

p. 84: the poem "Beauty Mark" owes a debt to "Beauty Spot" by Will Schutt, *Westerly*, Yale University Press, 2013.

p. 85: *two shores refuse to touch* comes from "Hunchback" by Alda Merini, Trans. Will Schutt, *Westerly*, Yale University Press, 2013.

p. 86: *We use water to start over* comes from "a lost line from a lost poem" by Colin Channer, unpublished, used with permission by the author.

p. 86: *fast & beautiful* comes from "What We Know of Horses" by Reginald Dwayne Betts, *Bastards of the Reagan Era*, Four Way Books, 2016.

p. 88: *I do not have a big dream they are only little dreams and right now I cannot think of one* comes from an interview with Eulina Costa Aluis of Cuba, *Women in the Material World* by Faith D'Aluiso and Peter Menzel, Sierra Club Books, 1996.

p. 89: *If I had to live under a bridge my children would go with me,* comes from an interview with Maria dos Anjos Ferreira of Brazil, *Women in the Material World* by Faith D'Aluiso and Peter Menzel, Sierra Club Books, 1996.

p. 95: *I swear by all flowers* comes from "since feeling is first" by E. E. Cummings, *The Complete Poems: 1904-1962 by E. E. Cummings*, Ed. George J. Firmage.

p. 96: *neutralizing ray* is how Tina Fey once described television.

p. 100: *go out for sweets & come back* comes from "summer, somewhere" by Danez Smith, *Don't Call Us Dead*, Graywolf Press, 2017.

p. 105: *If you can't be free, be a mystery* comes from "Canary" by Rita Dove, *Grace Notes*, W. W. Norton & Company, Inc., 1989.

p. 106: *sex and death and thinking* is a variation of a line from *Swimming Pool* by Jennifer Firestone, Doublecross Press, 2016.

p. 109: *Jenny's Woods* is what poet Karen Donovan told me she used to call a stand of trees that I can see from my kitchen window. As a child, Karen lived in the house across the way from my current home. Many of the trees are gone, but somehow the woods remain.

ACKNOWLEDGEMENTS

The following poems have appeared, in various forms, in the following journals:

"Reality Series," *Hanging Loose*, #75, 1999

"(My) American Journal," *The Literary Review*, Spring 2019

"(Y)our) American House," *Love's Executive Order*, July 2018

"Some Kinds of Fire," *Barrow Street*, Fall 2001

"Beauty Mark," *The Cortland Review*, Spring 2018

"Work" and "Hack," *The Common*, on-line Poetry Feature, Spring 2018

"Youngest Son," *The Good Men Project*, on-line, December 11, 2017

"Daily Beast," *The Good Men Project*, February 9, 2015

"Body of Water," *The Broome Street Review*, Spring 2017

"Handwork," *The Common*, Fall 2018, print edition

THANKS

to the editors who have supported my work through publication and otherwise:
Michael Morse of *The Literary Review*, Matthew Lippman of *Love's Executive Order*, John Hennessy at *The Common*,
Ginger Murchinson of *The Cortland Review*, Charlie Bondhus at *The Good Men Project*, Andrew Colarusso of *The Broome
Street Review*, Wyn Cooper, and, from way back, the editors at *Barrow Street* and *Hanging Loose*.

to the following people for friendship, love, and support in all its forms:
Michael Morse, Matthew Lippman, Greg Pardlo, Colin Channer, Matthew Zapruder, Orlando White, Michael Klein,
Dave Arons, In and Tim, Samantha Hirsch, Susan Gunter, Kristin Lehouillier, Tanya Solberg, Mary Kim Arnold,
Amy Pickworth, Esther Solondz, Natalie Schapero, and my wonderful editor at Veliz Books, Laura Cesarco Eglin.

With loving memories of my dad, Edwin Cane.

This book is dedicated to my husband, Pete, and our three children,
Cormac, Alma, and Titian: *the one living poem I've made*.